KINGDOM GIVING

a new perspective on wealth

D1365019

JERRY WEAR

ISBN 0-9765594-8-X

Cover and text art by Hampton Creative, Tulsa, OK

Printed in the United States of America.

The Great Commission Foundation of Campus Crusade for Christ
100 Lake Hart Drive, #3600
Orlando, FL 32832

www.gcfccc.org

Table of Contents

Introduction...5

1. Where in the World is Ulaanbaatar?............................ 11

2. It's *Who* You Know...19

3. "I'm Not Dying With All This Money"..........................27

4. Somewhere Over the Commode...................................33

5. Think Outside the Boat..43

6. Generations of Lazy People..49

7. Spotlight: Sinners!...55

8. From Mustard Weeds to Millions................................63

9. Big Hearts, Deep Pockets..69

10. Dead Men Don't Write Checks...................................75

11. Making Lemonade..83

12. A Life-Giving Legacy...89

13. What Would Jesus Do?...97

14. You Guessed It.. 103

Afterword.. 109

Why Not Die Broke?

An Introduction

"My goal is to die completely broke!"

This is the joyful cry of many of the people you're about to meet in the pages of this book.

Sounds crazy?

No. These are not skid row bums who have no ambition ... these are people who have been astoundingly successful in their careers and businesses. People who have earned millions, or multiple millions, by hard work and perseverance. And they aren't spending irresponsibly and wildly, either: many of them are living in modest homes, driving older model cars, teaching their children and grandchildren to work hard and live right.

Yet when they depart this life, they hope to have a *zero balance* in their bank accounts.

If the timing is right, and their dreams all come true, they will have *given away* every dime they've made — given it toward Kingdom ministries, to bring the hope of Jesus Christ to the nations and people of the world.

They will have poured out their lives as an offering to the Lord they love, and their legacy won't be millions left to their children or their company ... it will be a legacy in heaven, an eternal one.

These are men and women who have learned to think beyond
this lifetime, to the life to come — and this is the conclusion they've
drawn: the amazing joy they receive from giving it all away is only
a *minor representation* of the joy they'll experience in eternity from
having served the Savior so faithfully.

This is a revolutionary way of looking at the world, and
particularly at the financial world, at your personal economy. And yet
it reflects the Scriptures. It's the example of the Savior who taught us
to pray for our daily bread and nothing more in the way of financial
success (Matthew 6:11).

Yet very few believers ever come to this stage of their spiritual
development: a mature faith which says, "All I have and all I am is
God's. I lose nothing in giving it all back to Him."

In this book, my desire is for you to experience the same kind
of joy, the same deeply rewarding level of Christian maturity, as the
people you're about to meet: people who have taken their gift for
business, their God-given talent and acumen, and used it in a unique
way — not to build for themselves storehouses of wealth, but to store
up treasure in heaven (Matthew 6:20), where it awaits their arrival
and the voice of the Savior, "Well done, good and faithful servant"
(Matthew 25:23).

I want you to experience the joy they feel not only in the *giving*,
but in the *generating* of this wealth, the adventure both of making

money *and* giving it away in order to advance the Gospel. Because truly, the making and the giving are an adventure in themselves.

As you'll see, these millionaires and multi-millionaires aren't content, for the most part, to sit back and write a check. They're on the frontlines of the ministries they support, taking mission trips, networking with other Christian businesspeople, partnering in real ways with destiny-shaping ministries like Campus Crusade for Christ.

The Great Commission Foundation facilitates tax-savvy giving to Campus Crusade ministries, so naturally in my position as President I've met many wonderful believers who are totally motivated by generosity and passionate about presenting Christ to the world. They're among the ones I want you to meet in this book. Most of them are supporting and partnering with Campus Crusade, an outreach that operates in 191 countries with more than 25,000 staff worldwide, representing an amazing diversity of ministries: the JESUS Film, Military Ministry, Global Aid Network, FamilyLife, Campus Ministry, Here's Life Inner City, and much more. The members of our "History's Handful" group each pledged or gave $1 million or more to impact entire people groups through these and other outreaches. These givers are on the ground with us, making ministry happen, bringing hope to the lost souls of the world. No wonder they're filled with joy at the prospect of giving all for the Gospel!

I think about Craig Lawrence. Here's a man who felt a burden for the nation of Mongolia, and 20 years ago answered the call when Campus Crusade for Christ founder, the late Dr. Bill Bright, asked him to go. He asked him not only to *fund* a new outreach when Mongolia first opened to the Gospel in the last century, but to *go*, to meet the one known Christian there and actually prepare the way for massive evangelistic outreach. Craig called together a group of friends, asked them to pray, asked them to come with him ... and the results of what they began in Mongolia two decades ago are simply beyond belief. It was the beginning of an exciting adventure that continues today, and continues to change lives by the power of the Gospel.

People like Craig, and the others you'll meet in these pages, are businesspeople. They understand ROI (return on investment), and they're looking for the best possible return. But they've come to realize that there's an even *bigger payoff* than dollars and cents. There's something that makes the heart sing and gets the blood pumping in a way that mere money can't do. It's the exhilaration of impacting a single soul, a family, a community, a whole nation with the Gospel, so that the people who are walking in darkness may see a great light (Isaiah 9:2).

This isn't a book about anything as dry and dusty-sounding as stewardship. This is a book about the living, breathing, laughing, dancing *joy* of being the good steward God intended you to be. You're about to encounter living avatars of passion for the Savior ... passion that results in Kingdom giving ... giving that multiplies exponentially through wise investment in ministries making a global impact. These are people who aren't content to amass a fortune and then give a huge gift when they die — why would they find joy in that? They want to experience the joy of giving now, while they're living. They want to be rich toward God today, rather than building bigger barns when they already have more than enough (Luke 12:18).

They would consider it a true tragedy to live as others do: to bank on giving your immense gift through estate planning, to be stingy with God today in hopes of being able to be generous tomorrow. Why not choose to give now, they would ask, while you can experience the exhilaration of giving? Yes, joy can be found in leaving a wise spiritual legacy that's carefully planned from a tax standpoint. Your Christian will or estate plan can surely make an impact after you go home to be with the Savior. But if estate planning is what you do *instead* of pursuing the day-to-day adventure of good stewardship — well, what's in it for you, *today*? This is the secret our friends in this book have discovered: the immense, deep, and lasting joy that comes from taking the adventure God sends your way *today*. The adventure of giving — of pouring out your life to the last drop in His service ... and dying broke with a smile on your face.

(And consider this, even the *secular world* has begun to embrace this idea — according to a June 16, 2010, online article at *Fortune Magazine*: "Bill Gates, Melinda Gates, and Warren Buffet are asking the nation's billionaires to pledge to give at least half their net worth to charity, in their lifetimes or at death. If the campaign succeeds, it could change the face of philanthropy.")

There's more than enough money in the hands of evangelical Christians today to accomplish the Great Commission. Whether we do what Jesus called us to do with all this money is another matter. When you and I join the ranks of people like the ones in this book, when we plunge headlong into the joy of Kingdom giving — the adventure of ministry through generosity and active involvement — it can and will happen.

Journey with me now ... and see that the adventure has already begun!

Chapter 1

Craig Lawrence

Where in the World is Ulaanbaatar?

Genghis Khan. Now there was a man.

Mongols were fierce in his day — they ruled a huge Eurasian empire.

Even after Genghis' death, when the empire broke up, mighty Mongol warlords held the pieces for three centuries before the massive Chinese empire rolled in and conquered. Still, Mongolians continued to fight for their independence, and with the help of the USSR in 1924, they gained it. It was not as sweet a victory as they desired, however, because the USSR set up a repressive Soviet-style communist government — which controlled the nation until the Soviet Union dissolved there in 1991.

The dissolution of the USSR was a moment of destiny for Genghis Khan's Mongolia ... and for Craig Lawrence of Sioux Falls, too.

Two weeks before the fall of communism in Mongolia, Craig was ill at ease, and praying:

"God, I feel all divided up into neat little pieces. Doing this and doing that. But I long for a place in your Great Commission that would engulf me. The battle for the souls of men and women is the greatest calling of eternity, and I don't have a place of call. Lord, would you grant to me a ministry which would become a *consuming passion?*"

Today he says: be careful what you pray for.

As soon as the news broke — Mongolia was no longer under communist rule — Dr. Bill Bright, founder of Campus Crusade for Christ, called Craig. His message was simple — and huge: "Communism has fallen in Mongolia. We have no one to take responsibility for reaching that distant land. I'm asking you to do it. Say *yes*."

Craig was stunned. He had only a vague idea of where Mongolia was, and would have been baffled to try to spell the name of the capital city, Ulaanbaatar, where Dr. Bright wanted him to go. But he agreed to pray about it. He had been asking God for a consuming passion. Was this it?

In prayer, Craig seemed to hear the voice of God, reiterating this message in his heart: "I want you to learn to love the people of Mongolia." Convinced that this could be his calling, his *consuming passion*, Craig decided to put it to the test. He would invite Dr. Bright to Sioux Falls to present the vision to a small group of his friends. After all, what were the chances that such a busy man and ministry head would actually fly to South Dakota for a personal appearance?

Pretty good, as it turned out.

"A week later, I stood with Bill in front of about 40 of my friends," Craig recalls today, "and told them I believed God wanted us — in little known Sioux Falls — to take His Great Commission seriously and to reach the nation of Mongolia.

"I've never had a night like that one. In a few moments, they pressed checks for $145,000 into my hands. Twenty-three said they would go with me to premiere the JESUS Film."

Dr. Bright and the leadership of Campus Crusade could tell Craig of only one Christian they knew of in the entire nation of Mongolia. The team they formed on that night would truly be going as missionaries into unknown territory.

It was an unforgettable moment in Craig's personal history ... but little did he know that it was also an historic moment for Mongolia. The very week his team arrived in Ulaanbaatar, delegates to a new constitutional convention had also converged on the city. They were tasked with writing a new constitution which would firmly establish democracy as Mongolia's new form of government. There would be free elections, human rights, and a Buddhist state church. More than half the people followed Lamaism, a form of Buddhism that honors learned lamas, or spiritual leaders. About 40% claimed no religion after years of communist oppression, but their traditional faith was Lamaism. In celebrating their newly won freedom to exalt their culture, Mongolian leaders were set to declare Buddhism the state religion. The Constitution's draft read, "The religion IS Buddhism." Thus, despite the fall of Communism, Mongolia would remain closed to the Gospel.

At this pivotal moment, God had arranged for Craig Lawrence and his team of 23 believers from Sioux Falls to arrive in Ulaanbaatar.

The team set about identifying influential government leaders and individually extending to each one a personal invitation to a showing of the JESUS Film.

"In one evening — one powerful, star-filled, sub-zero night in January 1991 — God's Holy Spirit swept into that nation to rewrite what men had written," Craig says. "We premiered the JESUS Film for 350 government leaders. They watched ... some cried ... Mongolia met the message of the Savior."

It was clear Craig and his team had made an impact — but what kind of impact, exactly? The very next morning, armed Mongolian guards arrived at Craig's hotel room door and demanded that he come with them.

Was he being arrested?

Had the presentation of the Gospel been too radical?

Was he being taken to jail or deported?

No. They led him to the capitol building, to a large office, where three Mongolian government officials waited. Craig stood before them.

"Why are you here?" one of them asked.

"We are men whose hearts have been changed by Jesus Christ," Craig began, telling about himself and the team. "When we asked Him where we should go to tell of His love, He sent us here. We are your servants."

"Well, then," the leader replied, "do you think this Jesus could help us write our constitution?"

In that moment, words of Scripture flashed through Craig's mind: "We are therefore Christ's ambassadors, as though God were making his appeal through us" (2 Corinthians 5:20). His response was confident: "We would be honored to help you in His name."

Some of the believers on Craig's team were lawyers, and amazingly, experts in constitutional law. They set to work with the Mongolian government leaders, and actually helped write a constitution appropriate to a democracy — including the critical guarantee for citizens to have freedom of conscience and *freedom of religion.* Mongolia would be open to the Gospel by federal law ... all because, Craig says, "Campus Crusade had a leader who modeled faith and sacrifice, and because the JESUS Film had been produced and, in faith, translated into Mongolian ... and because God loves His people on earth. All glory, honor, and praise belong to Him. This bald-headed man from Sioux Falls feels privileged to have been part of it.

"Before we left Mongolia, the constitution was passed unanimously, hereby opening the door to a wave of missionaries who share in God's wonderful harvest at the ends of the earth."

The new, faith-friendly constitution was only the beginning.

"We've just finished our 950th prayer meeting for the people of Mongolia," Craig says today. "For the last 19 years, our little group has watched God build His Church in that distant land — from one known believer, to more than 50,000."

Craig and his band of friends formed AMONG Foundation to begin and support Christian programming in Mongolia.

Eagle TV is the first and only Christian television station in Mongolia, and, in fact, on the Asian continent, fully dedicated to advancing faith and freedom. The work that was begun in 1992 continues on in the media, but more importantly, in the lives of those who have found Christ as a result.

Chapter 2

—— Bill & Bobbie Crawford ——

It's *Who* You Know

Bill Crawford never cared a thing for NASCAR before.

Today he's a big fan.

What made the difference?

He went to the same high school as driver Jimmie Johnson. His little brother was friends with Jimmie — and Bill himself has the cherished memory of having raced in a go-cart against Jimmie Johnson back in the day. So when Jimmie came to prominence on the race track, it sparked a genuine interest in NASCAR ... because now, Bill had a personal connection.

Bill and his wife Bobbie have the same kind of personal connection to the ministries they support. It's a connection that has guided them to pour hundreds of thousands of dollars in charitable giving into those outreaches. Like a crisis pregnancy center started by personal friends. Shadow Mountain Church in the San Diego area. The Turning Point ministry of their pastor, Dr. David Jeremiah… and many others. Ask Bill and Bobbie and they'll tell you it's the personal connection with missionaries, ministers, and leaders that gives them the confidence to give ... confidence that their generosity is being wisely used, and producing the best possible return.

The idea was foreign to them, though, at first. Giving away thousands, even hundreds of thousands, of dollars? No way. Bill grew up in the Catholic Church but failed to connect personally with Jesus Christ. "Back then," Bill remembers, "if you saw me at mass on

Sunday and then at work on Monday, you probably wouldn't believe this was the same person."

But one Easter Sunday, some dear friends invited Bill and Bobbie to Shadow Mountain Church — so the Crawfords went to an early mass, and then to church with their friends.

"We were really blown away by this church," Bill remembers, "by the message from Pastor Jeremiah — and the people, how friendly they were. Having never been in a Baptist church before, we were overwhelmed."

"I was not raised with any religion in my family," Bobbie says. "When I married Bill, I knew for us to succeed as a couple we had to be alike as far as religion. I went through the Catholic Church training, I was baptized, confirmed, and went to church every Sunday. But once we went to Shadow Mountain, from that day on I knew this was where I was supposed to be."

Bill and Bobbie both made a personal commitment to Christ; it was the summer of 1993. Early the next year, Dr. Jeremiah preached a series of sermons on stewardship, and a whole new world opened up to the Crawfords.

"This was the first time I had heard the word *tithe* — never been exposed to it before," Bill says. "I just did not know what it was. Listening to David Jeremiah talk, I was very inspired by the teaching and by what the Bible had to say about it."

The Crawfords decided right then to begin tithing, at the beginning of 1994. One might expect it to be a struggle for businesspeople who had never before heard the word *tithe*. In fact, Bill says he knows his friends would have been aghast if they had known that every week, the first check he wrote was 10% of the gross from his paycheck — for the church! But because they were so excited about their new faith, and all that Christ had done for them, Bill and Bobbie never felt any pinch in tithing to their church. The new commitment even seemed to draw them into deeper closeness with Jesus.

Bill always prayed on the way to work, and he typically spent 15 minutes or so, in the parking lot before work, reading the Bible and praying. It was there that the idea came to him: "Bill, you own your own company. Why not work God into the company?" He knew now that he did not have to leave God at church on Sunday ... but he had never thought before about how to bring God into the workplace, too.

"Bobbie and I prayed for direction in working out the details of our new Christian business," Bill says. "We knew it was not necessary for everyone working at our business to be a Christian, but we wanted them to be on board with the direction we were going. We asked for God's help, if they were not committed, to remove them, or to make it evident to us that they didn't belong here. It really happened through God's grace that some people left, new people showed up, and we saw God working in our business."

It was around this time another idea began to form in Bill and Bobbie's minds: the idea that *all they had* was a gift from God ... that in fact, they didn't own their business, but God did! They began to tithe on the corporate profits in addition to tithing from their personal income. The profits were not large, so again, giving 10% might have been difficult — but they kept at it, and found that it gave them great joy!

And before long, the business needed more space!

Their business, Furniture Resources, provides "business furniture solutions." They'd been leasing space, but they had rapidly outgrown it as God prospered the company. Their banker showed them that if they leased a larger space, they'd end up paying $2 million for rent. Or they could take the same amount of money and buy their own building — a custom-designed permanent home for the business. Clearly, buying was the way to go. But they would need money for a down payment, and they had very little, considering all the costs of doing business *plus* the 10% they were giving away from the profits each month.

"We found a piece of dirt," Bill recalls, "a parcel of land that I actually sat in my truck on and prayed about." It seemed perfect for them, but the land's owners — who were members of their church, as it turns out — said they'd already accepted an offer; they advised the Crawfords to look elsewhere. "Then months later, we got a call from them," Bill says, "wondering if we were still interested in this property.

What they thought was a solid offer — fell through. We think God's hand was in it, and He had plans for us."

The Crawfords decided to purchase the land and build their own building ... and, while Bill never had doubts about tithing, he *did* have doubts about how they would come up with the down payment and the funding to build.

"I was having doubts and wanted to back out," Bill says. "I would say to Bobbie, 'This was a 7-digit deal, not 6 or 5 like we were used to carrying.' But she had complete peace about the deal, complete confidence that God would take care of us. With the grace of God, He filled up our bank account, and He made it happen for us."

The new facility gave the company room to grow — and it did: it's five times the size it was when they moved. ("Five times the amount we can tithe!" Bill says enthusiastically.) Today his commitment to taking steps of faith doesn't waver. He's seen God prove Himself faithful too many times.

"That showed us that God was part of our business, and that we had made the right decision to tithe the corporate profits," Bill says. "God is at the helm, in control, and we know our job is to be humble, responsible, and a good steward with those blessings that He gives us. We know He does not give us those resources to squander on ourselves. Tithing the company profits is a huge blessing."

Today, their company's website extols their commitment to honor

God and do business by biblical principles: "Honor, trust, God, and company! It may sound like the creed of one of the U.S. military branches, but in actuality, these are the fundamental principles used in the management philosophy at Furniture Resources ... From hiring personnel to interacting with clients, the Crawfords have been practicing these core values since the company was first incorporated in 1992. To date they have never led them astray."

With greater profits providing greater resources from which to give, the Crawfords have found greater joy in helping more ministries, too. "We are personally connected to where those resources go," Bill says. "For instance, to the friends who started the pregnancy center, to Motor Racing Outreach where a friend is a chaplain, and to friends who started a new outreach project. Of course our church, and Turning Point ... the Turning Point mission is really easy to grab hold of. Get God's Word out, His message of salvation to everyone and everywhere. It is God's commandment to us to participate in something that directly follows His Great Commission. You don't have to wonder what they are going to do, or what they will do with the resources given; you just know."

Bill and Bobbie have no regrets about the way they've poured their personal finances and corporate profits into ministries that are proclaiming the good news of Jesus Christ and helping people find hope and a future. In fact, they encourage every business owner who loves Jesus to do the same.

"You don't need to stand up on a soapbox and be an evangelist yourself," Bill says. "If those values and examples that Christ modeled for all of us can be put into your business, you cannot help but have God's presence at work. Then I think tithing from your business is just a natural step for you — keeping in mind that it's not just about tithing the corporate profits, it's about — how do I put Christ into my business, every day, every minute, and every hour?"

Bill and Bobbie have figured out how to do it, and their godly leadership of the business they own has made a tremendous difference — not only on their balance sheet, but for a world in need, because they've embraced a corporate lifestyle of generosity.

Chapter 3

—— Denny and Sally Foster ——

"I'm Not Dying
With All This Money"

Denny Foster's goal is to be dead broke ... or, more accurately, broke and then dead.

His wife, of course, supports him in this dream, but like many wives and mothers, she also has a need for security, enough money to sustain them in their old age. What would make Denny completely happy would be a blueprint of their lives, so he could know the exact moment to give away the last of their money, and then awaken in the presence of Christ, having poured themselves out in His service. But Denny knows, from years in the construction and development business, that there's no such blueprint.

So his plan, with Sally's blessing, is just to keep on working, keep on giving, keep on taking risks for the Gospel, and leave the rest in God's hands.

"Spiritual gifts," says Sally reflectively. "What do you do when one member of your marriage has one spiritual gift and the other has another? Denny loves to give; this is his spiritual gift. So I have to back off and allow Denny to give, and give, and give."

With this understanding, the Fosters have been able to give millions to Kingdom works, and they plan to do even more in the future. What drives this generosity?

"It would be impossible to imagine not having Christ as part of my life," Denny says. "Everything I do and say, well, I just cannot even imagine living life without Christ. So when I hear about people who don't know Christ, it makes me sad, that they don't have the joy that comes with knowing Him."

Sally agrees. And she's on board because of what she has seen on the mission field herself.

"I think the things that impacted me the most," she says, "are seeing or hearing about people living in places like India and Somalia dealing with poverty and starvation; they live in such difficult circumstances. We go through difficult times, but because God loves us we know we have all that we need."

Having all you need seems to be the key in their plans — plans to give away everything they *don't need*. Surprisingly, what many people see as near-necessities have been joyfully pushed to the back-burner by the Fosters.

Denny recalls the teaching of Randy Alcorn, author of the popular book *The Treasure Principle*: "Live at a level that you are comfortable with, and then stay at that level, and do not get a bigger car, bigger house. And Randy lives that out. We try to do that, too. In fact, we had a missionary friend who loved to come stay at our home because he said we always had the same couch, the same car — comfortable, but not extravagant.

"To me, it is also about breaking it down to the lowest common denominator," Denny says. "It is an investment, and it is picking the best investment that gives the greatest return. With the JESUS Film

Project, we have a great return on our investment: for every dollar, six to 10 people will hear the Gospel, and historically one or more will come to know Christ.

"Then when you begin to evaluate your own expenses, your expenditures, you think, 'I have a choice of adding a pool, which will cost $30,000 to $40,000, and I will have the enjoyment of the pool. Or I can give the money so that 40,000 people can have the opportunity to come to know Christ.' If you look at it this way, how in the world would you ever make a decision to spend your money in such a self-centered way?"

With logic like this, it's no surprise Denny's dream is to die broke.

But what about his family?

The Fosters' two adult sons have also caught the spirit of giving. Year by year as they were growing up, they heard their father suggesting, "Let's skip Christmas presents this year and give the money to missions." They understand a heart for missions, and they're not upset by their parents' desire to pour everything into the Kingdom.

"The boys understand that they will not get some gigantic inheritance, so that they can go out and buy a Mercedes," Sally says. "They know, and they agree, and they are both givers."

Some people might think it's easy for a multi-millionaire land developer to give away money and still have plenty to live on. But the Fosters don't live an extravagant lifestyle. (Denny calls himself "God's

Handyman," which is appropriately down-to-earth for him.) They
have too much regard for the Kingdom to be extravagant ... although
sometimes they may be tempted.

"It's a struggle," Sally says. "We could live right on the beach, by
the ocean. I would love to live on the beach, and would love a pool out
in the yard; but I'm not getting any of that. When I get discouraged,
I remember where the money really needs to go, and it is actually
thrilling, just thrilling to give — to think about the impact you have on
the world.

"Movie stars are going to give money to causes dealing with health
issues," she adds, "but they are not going to change someone's heart.
We give so that others can live eternally with God. We want to see
these people in heaven, not because we know them, but because of the
thrill of being a part of the community of Christ."

The thrill of giving, of knowing that their investment means eternal
joy for those who may never yet have heard the story of Jesus Christ,
is an exhilaration not to be rivaled by pools, or cars, or beach houses.
Denny wholly believes God has blessed him with a job he loves, and
success in business, so that he can be a blessing to others. And Sally
relates their missions giving to her own life:

"You have to look at your life, how you were changed because
someone invested in you, and someone invested in my life, too," she
says. "Someone had a vision to invest their money to show me a Billy

Graham movie back when I was 19. Someone gave up their time to explain to me about Jesus, and now my life is changed forever. I see the value in this change, and I just feel, what a privilege to help change *someone else's life in this way!*"

"I remember we were involved with a group of international students here," Denny says. "We were asked to pick up this boy from India and take him to an event. I asked him if he had ever heard of Jesus, and he said, 'Yes, I remember seeing this film about Jesus, when I was a little boy, sitting in my mother's lap.' Sally and I looked at each other, and instantly we knew: 'Wow! Maybe our money went toward that film he watched!' That's the payoff, that's the value of giving.

"And it's greater than you can even imagine!"

Chapter 4

Somewhere
Over the Commode

Take a look at the toilet — well, OK, just *above* the toilet. There's a plaque. With a fellow's name. It's the only recognition he wanted for all he has invested in various ministries of Campus Crusade for Christ. He had commented to the leader of one of our most influential ministries about philanthropists who wanted their names on hospital wings or important buildings — his sense of humor resulted in the plaque over the ministry leader's toilet.

This giver doesn't want any fuss made about him or his generosity. He doesn't even want me to use his name in this story. So, for this story, we'll just call him John. That seems appropriate, right? In fact the whole men's room metaphor might continue: if you look at John's net worth from a worldly viewpoint, you might think it's going down the toilet — because it's shrinking. Most businesspeople would be alarmed by this state of affairs, but not John. In fact, he's the architect of it: he's trying to give it all away. He comes from a wealthy family, but since he came to know Christ, he's separated many of his business affairs from theirs — so he can be more liquid, and give as generously as he likes, any time he likes.

John's commitment to ministry and building God's Kingdom goes far beyond his outrageous generosity. He's using his business skills to help launch new ministries, streamline and organize existing ones, and network with others who can support these outreaches.

"At first I thought I would just write checks," he recalls. He had not been a Christian very long, and he was only beginning to investigate what stewardship meant, and how to give strategically.

His wife, who had been a Christian for some time before John came to know Christ, had long supported a Campus Crusade staff member — which at the time he had thought to be ludicrous. But now that he, too, knew the importance of sharing God's love, he wanted to help. John visited many different churches and researched many different ministry organizations, always looking for the best return on investment (ROI). He and his wife had attended a Campus Crusade Executive Briefing, and he was inspired by the late Dr. Bill Bright's presentation — as founder of Campus Crusade, he was well able to present the whole scope of the vision.

"Paul Eshleman also spoke about the distribution of the Gospel that was already in place, and this appealed to me as a businessman," John says. "I wasn't giving to build the infrastructure, it was already there."

John was further moved by the next speaker, who described the JESUS Film Project. Next up: a speaker from Thailand.

"The speaker from Thailand was pretty boring," John recalls with a smile, "but he said two things that caught my attention: what his annual budget was, and how many people were coming to Christ that year. I did the math on a cloth napkin." John discovered that Crusade was "snagging these Christians at 31 cents a pop." John immediately said to himself, "I want a piece of that."

But he thought he would only write checks.

Some people may be able to "just write checks" and make a huge impact! We're really grateful for people like that. But John had so much more to offer, it wasn't long before his role as a volunteer adviser, consultant, and organizer became just as important as his generous giving. The Campus Crusade director of the ministry in North Africa and the Middle East recognized how John's strengths could be utilized and invited him to be on their team. When John finally accepted, he found himself part of the team planning the budget and outreaches for the region.

"It finally occurred to me," John says today, "if I gave to the leadership largely undesignated, I could become part of the team and it would not be me deciding the project. If I believe in the leadership, and give to the leadership undesignated, it would take the onus off me, and it would free us up to be more peers — money can get in the way."

John and his wife have continued to narrow the focus of their Campus Crusade giving to "NAMESTAN," the strategic region that encompasses North Africa, the Middle East, and the Central Asian Republics — where there are cultures that are traditionally antagonistic toward Christianity. While they continue to invest dollars generously, John has helped in completing an overhaul of Campus Crusade's organizational systems in these areas.

"It was a task force for regionalization, changing the structure of NAMESTAN's leadership," John explains. The goal: "There would be extra regional directors, so that not all the countries report to one person. We were creating a detailed plan — not just dividing it up into regional directors, but to plan how to communicate it to all the stakeholders while including them in the process."

The process was important because of the nature of ministry in these countries and regions: "People out there can feel very alone," John observes. "These are tough countries, and contact is not always easy; and it can feel like you are very alone. Interacting with your peers and your superior isn't always available, especially if your superior has 30 people reporting to him." The new structure he helped to develop will alleviate stress on the individual staff and on the supervisors as well.

This project represents just one of four task forces John handled for the NAMESTAN region over the years. His skills and expertise have come to be relied upon by the leadership. John recognizes that his business and networking experience helped him in this area, too. "What I am best at," he says, "is if you want to get something started, get something going. I can be quite a bit of help in this area."

Today, John and his wife give away more than 50% of their income. Basically, he says, they set aside what they need to live for a year, plus money to pay taxes; then they give away the rest. At this giving level, not all of what they give is tax-deductible each year, but John has resisted the idea of forming a foundation that would administer their giving.

"If we did, it would be counter-productive to what I want to do, since with a foundation you can only put in 30% tax-free — and I am using over 50% of the funds. It seems to me that private foundations are sometimes set up when a family wants to control and prolong their giving."

John and his wife haven't felt the need to closely control where their giving is going, since they've come to know and trust the leaders in the three main areas where their giving is concentrated. In fact, this is one of their three principles for charitable giving:

- Go *narrow*. Pick only a few areas of giving, and give enough to make a real impact in each one.
- Go *deep*. Give relationally: know and trust the people, not the project. If you know the heart of the leader you're investing with, you can more easily overcome any bumps in the road.
- Go *long*. Commit to the leadership and not necessarily to individual projects, allowing relational giving to carry into the future without interruption. When the leadership knows they can count on you, trust is enhanced.

What about those "bumps in the road" which do occasionally happen, where a project doesn't pan out as intended, or a staff member can't go the distance after all?

"Bad things happen in ministry sometimes," John admits. He has experienced it himself. "But when it goes bad, let's get it fixed. We have relationships with the leaders. But one mistake is not a reason to stop giving. Bad things happen in a family and the family stays together. We are going to find a way to stay in the relationship, and how to continue. If they have good leaders and mistakes happen, and unforeseen things happen, let's get over it and on with it."

In fact, this approach is pivotal in light of what is called the "Great Commandment" of Christ: "Love the Lord your God with all your heart and with all your soul and with all your strength and with all your mind; and, Love your neighbor as yourself" (Luke 10:27).

"The Great Commandment should be driving the Great Commission," John says. "The Great Commandment is very much about relationship with others, and if you have a strong relationship, you will go the distance."

John and his wife also support Mars Hill Graduate School in Seattle, another ministry dear to their hearts. Mars Hill offers Master's degrees in Counseling, Christian Studies, and Divinity. John regards the school as offering a great return on investment, since it is sending workers into the harvest. This is what investing in ministry is really all about, as John has had to remind himself from time to time.

"I was an arrogant donor," he says. "My wife and I were giving substantial amounts of money and time. We were giving to individuals, to ministries like Campus, FamilyLife, East Asia, NAMESTAN, plus lots of others. Everyone loves to see you. But I realized I was arrogant about my role. I knew I was helping a lot of people. I knew they were counting on me, and there is a certain amount of pride that you are carrying a heavy load."

A bad year in business made it clear to John that he wouldn't be able to give *anything* to NAMESTAN the following year. When a rep called to check on him, John asked the rep to break this distressing news to the area director, who of course had come to rely on John's investment each year. Somehow, the message was never given to him. At the annual summit to plan the budget and outreaches, another friend asked John if he'd be able to *increase* his giving that year. When he heard that John could give nothing, his face fell. "Oh. I see. We'll have to tell the director...."

John was humbled, really humiliated, but he knew he had to be the one to break the bad news.

"How could I be so arrogant that I could not even talk to a friend about the fact that I did not have the money this particular year?" John says today. "I immediately got convicted by the Lord, about how arrogant I was, how awful it was, and how deeply I was moved about it all."

Giving without pride, simply for the joy of being able to extend God's Kingdom, has become the new standard for John and his wife.

Their children are excited about it, too. "They always say they're not counting on me for an inheritance," John says. "Our family is quite wealthy, but we are using up a lot. My personal net worth is decreasing, not increasing, and I am fine with that. And my children are fine with that. And they know what they *do* receive from me, I want them to give away."

His advice for anyone who is struggling about when, how, and where to give?

"Get relationally connected, know the leaders, care for the leaders, and trust will abound — then it becomes a *get to* and not a *got to*!"

Chapter 5

—— Ed and Wanda Thomas ——

Think Outside the Boat

Houston was a happening place before the oil bust.

The housing market was growing, oil money was flowing, and for enterprising real estate developers like Ed Thomas, the construction business was booming. That was back in the early '80s. Then oil went to $10 a barrel, and the bottom dropped out of the Houston economy — with results that are eerily similar to recent years. Housing foreclosures, job loss, and for real estate developers like Ed Thomas, half-built or empty buildings that wouldn't be finished or occupied for years, if ever, were bleeding money where they stood.

"My wife, Wanda, and I were on the verge of bankruptcy," Ed remembers. "In addition, we had personal liability of several million dollars on developments that were almost empty."

Then God, with His perfect timing, reconnected Ed with an old football buddy from college. His buddy invited him to a Campus Crusade for Christ World Briefing Conference. Since he hadn't seen his friend in years, Ed agreed to go — although he knew very little about Campus Crusade, and of course, had no money to give.

"What happened there changed my life, and the way I look at business and money," Ed says today. "I learned that $1 would reach 6 people with the JESUS Film in their language, and, historically, 1 of the 6 would accept Christ. We were given the challenge that if 1,200 businesspeople would pledge $1 million, we could fulfill the Great Commission. I came back to Houston pumped up, and told my wife about it, and she said the obvious: '*We don't have $1 million.*'"

Just a few years before, writing a check for a million dollars would have been well within their grasp. But at this time in their lives, it seemed like an impossible dream. Still, Ed couldn't get the idea out of his head: a million souls, saved for eternity. His wife agreed to pray about the idea ... and felt the Lord leading her to the same conclusion: they were to be among the 1,200 who would commit $1 million.

"When we stepped out in faith to make that commitment," Ed says, "God opened up a door which has led to the most exciting adventure of our lives. Faith is simply believing in God, getting Him involved and trusting Him for the results — just like the Apostle Peter when he saw Jesus walking on the water."

Ed loves that story from Matthew 14 — especially because all the disciples saw Jesus walking on the water, but only Peter had the faith to ask whether he, too, could do it.

"Peter, when he saw Jesus walking on the water, climbed out of the boat to do something supernatural with Jesus," Ed observes. "The other disciples saw the supernatural taking place but were fearful of the surrounding circumstances and chose to stay in the boat. As long as Peter had his eyes on Jesus, he *did* the supernatural!"

Ed and Wanda climbed out of the boat — they stopped focusing on the storm of their financial circumstances and instead plugged into God's power. And just like Peter, who was able to walk on the water as long as his eyes stayed focused on Jesus, Ed and Wanda began to experience the supernatural.

"Not only did God resolve our financial dilemma, but He provided the resources to fulfill our $1 million pledge," Ed says. "Right now, He's providing for our *third* $1 million gift, to Campus Crusade and other Kingdom endeavors — such as Global Media Outreach and Faith Comes By Hearing, which have tremendous eternal leverage for every dollar." Global Media Outreach is a CCC ministry that annually reaches millions of people with the Gospel worldwide through the Internet. Faith Comes By Hearing is an international Scripture mission that provides God's Word in audio form in the heart-language of unreached people groups worldwide. In many countries, it is a big part of the follow-up and discipleship for the JESUS Film.

But the Thomas' influence doesn't end at giving money; in fact, it just begins there. Because God has so abundantly blessed them financially, and has given Ed a tremendous gift for business and for generating wealth, doors are opening around the world for him to speak and teach. He's visited 57 nations, and in the course of sharing with national CEOs and businesspeople, Wanda and he have also shared their faith hundreds of times.

"I believe that God desires for each Christian businessperson to involve God in the business," Ed says, "to step out in faith, and open an exciting door to a new journey with Christ. I was in my late

40s when God started me on this adventure, and I've never looked back." He has even adopted the acronym History's Handful uses for businesspeople to give their "LIFE" for the Kingdom:

L *Labor.* Use the special talents that have enabled you to become a success in the world's eyes. Your business can become a Kingdom business! Organizations like "The CEO Institute" have been formed to help you operate biblically and become a part of the "Business as Mission" movement.

I *Influence.* Use your network of contacts to open doors and get impossible things done. The business community has the most influence of any sector in the world. Doors of business and government leaders are open to discuss business and entrepreneurship.

F *Finances.* This is cash flow, or the treasure you have stored up. The dollars in your pocket are your seed — don't be a foolish farmer and refuse to plant. This includes net worth, your non-cash assets, as well. You can't take it with you, but you can invest it for eternal blessings.

E *Expertise.* Your skills and experience are needed, especially in the undeveloped world. God wants to use the Christian business community to change the economies of nations and elevate poor people worldwide. The knowledge you've gained is critical to this.

"Business owners and CEOs share a common DNA: the money-making genes," Ed says. "I used to feel bad about it: why was I so focused on making money? But then God showed me: He uniquely designed me that way. He wants me to think about money and how to make money, but with one major focus: for His pleasure and His glory."

Perhaps you, too, have been uniquely designed to focus on money and how to make more. If so, Ed's message for you is the same one the Holy Spirit has driven home to him:

"God truly does want you to climb out of the boat, plug into His power, and use your LIFE (labor, influence, finances, and expertise) for His glory," Ed says. "I have personally made the decision that it is 'pedal to the metal' for Christ in the years I have remaining, and I encourage you to do the same. Turn temporal success into eternal *significance* in the years, months, and days that remain for you."

Chapter 6

—— Mike and Sheila Ingram ——

Generations of Lazy People

Generations of lazy people — that's what Mike and Sheila Ingram want to avoid: using their wealth to raise children who don't understand hard work and won't even try.

"My wife and I started out with nothing, and we will leave the same way," Mike says. "We feel that leaving all of our money to our children creates generations of lazy people." Instead, they're teaching their children how to provide for themselves, and how to be givers — which is really the best investment of all.

As for Mike and Sheila themselves, Mike says, "Our estate plan is simple: give it all away to ministries, and there will be no taxes."

The giving habit started early in Mike's life. His father died when he was young, so Mike was raised by a single mom, a strong believer. She taught him that "you can't out-give God." Mike tithed on his pay from the very first jobs he held; but that was only the beginning.

"We are not limited to just 10% giving," Mike says. "After all, giving always brings back returns. It is not about how much you are giving, it is where your heart is. No one can buy their way into heaven ... but the more you give, the more you are blessed."

As a successful land developer, Mike was greatly blessed in business. His generosity overflowed to ministries like FamilyLife, the JESUS Film Project, and other global outreaches. But much more than writing a check, his personal involvement on mission trips to India, South America, Russia, and Romania, and his work planting two new churches, have taught him about the impact he's making.

"Mission trips gave me insight about the value of money and our priorities," Mike says. "Now I think about things, like when I play golf — and I love to play golf — it's hard for me to look beyond the cost of playing golf. It usually costs about $125 to $150 for me to play, and then you add three others to the round, and it becomes $600. Then I think about what $600 could do in missions...."

The Ingrams count their personal involvement in a new church plant as perhaps the single most significant investment they've ever made.

"Church planting involves not just money but time, lots of time, and a big personal commitment, showing up every Sunday. No vacations, or very limited time off, in order to be in church on Sunday," Mike observes. "My wife probably worked 70-hour weeks during that time. But through it all, we grew in God's love. As we look back, those were the greatest times of our lives. Life-changing times. Spiritual growth. And very rewarding experiences."

The couple invests in several ministries and serves on the board of Pinnacle Forum, a group of community leaders focused on growing in their faith, networking with like-minded peers, and discovering how God wants to use them for His glory in promoting the values of Jesus Christ within the culture. A fellow Pinnacle Forum board member is Jerry Colangelo, former owner and current chairman of the Phoenix

Suns basketball team. Together, Mike and Jerry chair the NFL-
sanctioned Super Bowl Breakfast the day before the big game — an
event that helps spotlight exemplary character, values, and faith in the
professional sports arena.

Mike says the key to choosing where to invest your charitable
giving is in getting to know and trust the leadership.

"Leadership in the ministry is the answer," he advises.

"Establish a relationship with the leadership, and then get involved
in the ministry, believe in the program. Finances are also important:
there are lots of great ministries out there, so take a look at the
ministry's overhead, its benefits and non-essential spending; consider
every aspect. And then stay connected. Remember that change will
happen whenever the Lord is at work, so be prepared for changes, and
just stick with it."

Mike has been influenced by the book *Half Time* by Bob Buford.
"The book talks about going from success to significance. It teaches
us a great message, especially for us mid-life guys: we can use our
business as a platform for influence. We want to use that platform
to spotlight Christ." This is something Mike and Sheila have done,
despite their own recent business setbacks.

The global economic crisis has hampered Mike's business; for two
years the family has been living on their savings. While it's not their
first choice, they're finding the faith to carry on and grow, despite the

circumstances.

"Money comes and goes, and we are here for a short time," Mike says. "We continue to live by this lesson we learned a long time ago: none of this money is ours; it is God's for us to use and give away."

The Ingrams' ability to give mega-amounts has been impacted by the economic downturn, but not their commitment to ministry — and their desire to keep giving all they can.

Chapter 7

Norm Miller

Spotlight: Sinners!

Look at Norm Miller, successful, respectable, 72-year-old southern white Christian....

You don't expect the website he helped co-found to feature people like the tattooed metal musician Brian Welch, former lead singer of the heavy-metal band Korn, once renowned for its explicit lyrics and the immoral lifestyles of its musicians. In fact, this crazy website, iamsecond.com, features an array of sinners who freely talk about having an abortion, having an affair, abusing drugs and alcohol —

And then they tell about how the love of Christ saved and transformed them.

The site, www.iamsecond.com, was launched in December of 2008 as Miller's effort to reach his "Jerusalem," the Dallas/Ft. Worth metroplex with the good news. But the site receives thousands of hits from all over the world, people hungry to know that no life is beyond redemption — which is exactly what you discover through the site's videos, spotlighting both celebrities and everyday people. Norm understands this as well as anyone: he was once caught in the throes of alcoholism. But after he surrendered his life to Christ, he stopped drinking and immersed himself in church and Bible studies. As he grew in his walk with the Lord, he came to realize how critical it is to give to Kingdom work, and that giving is an act of obedience and worship, i.e. the lifting up of CHRIST.

"As a Christian, I was moved by Scriptures like Luke 12:18,"

Norm says, "where the foolish man talks about building bigger barns to store more of his possessions. And 1 John 3:17, about having pity for a brother in need. Or Jesus' commandment in Matthew 5:40 — that if someone demands your shirt, you should give him your coat as well. My thinking was that, if someone asks me for something, or if I saw a need and God touched me about it, I would try to do it. I'm a businessman, so I know the army has to eat, the workers have to be fed."

This attitude has led Norm into an adventure in giving spanning four decades — with no signs of stopping. One of the first Bible studies Norm ever participated in, just two weeks after coming to Christ, was a Bill Bright seminar on how to share your faith. He's been involved in Campus Crusade ministries ever since, in addition to supporting many other missionaries, churches, outreaches, and organizations across the USA and around the world. His position as Chairman of the Board for Interstate Batteries has provided the resources for this extreme generosity. It's also provided a bully pulpit for Norm and his team to share God's love.

The "I Am Second" website and media campaign represent just one recent outreach to Dallas/Ft. Worth. Others have included an animated commercial for local markets that extolled God's love and how transformative it can be.

"One morning in March of 2008," Norm recalls, "I was thinking about turning 70 in the summer, and wondering how much longer

I would be here. I had made the 3 score and 10! I began to think of Dallas/Ft. Worth as my Jerusalem, in terms of witnessing — in Acts 1:8 Jesus says, 'You will be my witnesses.' I have been all over the world spreading the Word, but I have never gone for broke here in "my" home area. In my mind I thought, *I need to spread the message of Christ, to spread the truth to the North Texas area. If I don't do it, there will be people who do not hear the message.*"

The website, co-founded by e3 Partners, launched in cooperation with 20 local churches and a toll-free call-for-help number, 800-NEED-HIM. Countless visits to the site and heartfelt responses have followed. e3 continues to add more inspiring video stories of transformed lives to the website all the time, sharing with the Dallas area, and the whole world, the power of God's love. Norm admits that maintaining a cutting-edge website is an expensive endeavor, but where Kingdom values are concerned, he and others now do not hold back.

For instance, at Interstate Batteries, he says, "We want to share the Gospel without being offensive, without the worry of losing employees, losing the business, or being sued. So we've had to get creative." During the Year of the Bible, when the U.S. Congress made a proclamation about the value of the Scriptures, Interstate Batteries sent a copy of the proclamation, along with a Bible, to each of their distributors. Another time they sent hundreds of people a free book by a Christian counselor about rearing teenagers. "It came with a memo that said we all struggle with teenagers, and hopefully this book will help. The response was very positive." Norm has sent exciting books by Christian authors to his company's dealers and employees, along with Christian music. Last year at their annual brunch event, the Newsboys performed, and there was an entire presentation of the Gospel and an invitation to receive CHRIST.

Norm doesn't stop with his business associates. There's even more to tell about how he and Interstate support missions and ministries at home and abroad. But how does a man with such resources and such a desire to give decide which people or organizations should receive his support? Norm has a simple checklist:

- Know the person.
- Know their heart.
- Agree it's a GOD pleasing mission.
- Understand what they want to accomplish.

"It wasn't a big deal at first, like starting out giving to Campus Crusade for Christ staff, or to a specific ministry," Norm recalls, "usually giving $15 or $25 a month, and as time went on more and more. I felt a responsibility to give, and that giving was an opportunity. God allows us to be investors. In John 15:16 Jesus says He has appointed us to bear fruit that will last — that's the 'proof' of our discipleship, the fruit. And in Jesus' parable about the talents in Matthew 25, it's the one who made a lot from a little who is commended and used. 'What have you done with what I gave you?' the Master asks. I take it as some kind of formula that we are to produce — make a prayerful effort to produce that which will increase God's Kingdom."

It makes sense, then, that Norm invests where he sees a mission being accomplished, lost souls finding hope in Christ, and lives transformed.

"It all comes down to prayer, too," he adds. "One of my prayers is for God to show me what He wants me to do for all those we support. And lately, I found in 1 Timothy 1:5, The goal of our instructions is to love from a pure heart, sincere faith, and clear conscience. So I am trying to make sure that my giving is based on loving God, loving others, and trying to further the Kingdom."

"Leveraging" is also an important word to Norm when he's considering where to invest his charitable giving. He supports Dallas Theological Seminary, for example, because "they graduate 300 students per year, and if only 65% end up in mission work for 30 years, then you have at least 200 going out teaching and preaching for 30 years. And this multiplies every year, since they are graduating another 300 potential pastors and missionaries every year!" THAT's phenomenal!

Another ministry, Overseas Council, offers Norm a similarly exciting ROI: "I'm on the board," he says, "and we help over 106 seminaries and Bible institutes in the non-Western world. We graduate 11,000 every year, and I have been involved with that for more than 20. The years of manned ministry are amazing. We know for a fact that 90% of the people stay in ministry for 20 to 30 years."

Any ministry offering such good leveraging attracts Norm's attention as a businessman, so naturally the JESUS Film Project is one of his long-time favorites. The film is cost-effective (6 people can see it for a dollar, and historically 1 of the 6 will make a commitment to Christ); plus, it's used in planting churches or to steer new believers into existing churches.

"I got in on the JESUS Film Project back in 1979-80, and just think about those multiples," Norm says with a gleam in his eye. "It's as if I'd gotten in on Apple when they first started. So the return in the furthering of God's Kingdom is phenomenal. I look at it not arrogantly, but I look at it as my answer to the Master when He asks, What have you done with what I gave you?"

So far, Norm has done a lot with what God gave him, and the ministries he's supporting are bearing the precious external fruit. That fruit is proof of his discipleship, proof of his love for the Savior and more importantly, proof that GOD will use any of us if we'll draw near to HIM and trust HIM in scripture-based, Holy Spirit-led giving obedience!

Chapter 8

—— *Paul and Ruth Lindholm* ——

From Mustard Weeds
to Millions

It was the Great Depression, and 10-year-old Paul Lindholm had his first job: picking yellow-flowered wild mustard weeds in the grain fields. When he had picked 10 dozen and left them at the end of the field, he got a dime. Almost.

"My father would set aside one penny — 'That's for the Lord' — and give me the other nine," Paul remembers. It was his first real introduction to tithing, a lesson that has stayed with him all his life.

"Back then my father gave 10%, even on the farm," Paul recalls. "Pretty soon, when times got better in the 1940s and '50s and '60s, and he was making more money, he didn't increase his lifestyle, but he *did* increase his giving.... My father gave 20, 30, 40, and even 50 percent of his income to the Lord."

That fatherly example instilled in Paul the desire to give. God gave him an equally strong desire to share his faith in Christ. Since the age of nine, he's been witnessing to friends and people he meets about the power of God to transform lives.

"I have always wanted to bring people to Christ, but I said to the Lord: *Don't let me mention the name of Jesus unless You first give me a love for the person, and let the person know I love them, and care for them, and am not judging them.*"

His prayers seem to be answered: Paul regularly shares his faith with his seat-mate on an airplane, or someone he meets on a walk around the neighborhood, or an audience member who hears him speaking during one of the mission trips he frequently makes. One such journey found him addressing 26 inmates in a women's prison in Paraguay, all of whom were hardened criminals, some even murderers.

"When I mentioned that God loved them as much as He loved me, I could just see what was going on — the tears coming into their eyes. They were stunned to hear this news," Paul remembers. "Then when I said a prayer of accepting Christ, asking them to pray silently in their hearts and mind, there was not silence, but the repeating of the interpreter's words — out loud, with weeping — all 26 of them."

Such experiences, which bring Paul great joy, are amazing but not uncommon. As he supports the JESUS Film Project, for example, he's helped to facilitate film showings in various locales, and he speaks to local leadership before the showings.

"In St. Petersburg, Russia, about 450,000 people came to see the JESUS Film," he recalls, "which was being shown in 100 theatres that Campus Crusade for Christ had rented. I was speaking at six different dinner events to a total of about 100 community leaders and representatives of the various theatres from the metropolitan area. Seventy of the 100 came to believe in Christ."

Because Paul is a successful banker, many doors have opened in other nations. In Santa Cruz, Bolivia, he was very much in demand to speak with city leaders, national bankers, and corporation heads. At the same time, local believers were holding prayer meetings and praying for these influential men and women to come to know Christ as Savior. At the end of this week-long outreach, Paul spoke at a banquet — and 225 of the city's government and corporate leaders came to Christ! Paul and his wife Ruth have such an intense personal ministry, it's easy to see why they want to support full-time missionaries and ministers, as well as other churches and organizations, who are sharing the Gospel in relevant and powerful ways. Their commitment — and ability — to give has increased dramatically over the years, but Paul keeps it all in an eternal perspective.

"You really have to get your eyes off the idea of money," he says. "When I was younger, of course I wanted to be a millionaire, but it was not a focus for me. Then when I became a millionaire, I thought I'd like to make a million dollars a *year* — and when that happened, I thought, 'I want to *give away* a million dollars a year!' And that is happening now. It came not because I had my eyes fixed on it, but because Ruth and I had our eyes fixed on Jesus. And that is what Jesus wanted us to do."

In addition to providing a source of income, owning the bank has put Paul and Ruth into a position of great influence in their community — and as owners, they are free to use the bank's name and resources to build God's Kingdom, too. Twice a month, the bank runs an ad in the local newspaper — it's actually an article by Paul, encouraging community service or publicizing a project. Very often Paul shares his faith in the article, too. Last Christmas, the bank's ad read:

Thoughts from a banker. . .

Those of us who have a job or business and are doing
well should give more to pick up the slack for those
who are struggling.

Difficult times should bring out the best in us.

He has certainly lived this message, and continues to, by
giving generously to a variety of outreaches like Military Ministry,
FamilyLife, and ministries in Eastern Europe and Africa.

"I think there is and should be urgency about giving," Paul asserts,
"and I think it is wise to give substantially when you are living and
earning — and not accumulate wealth in order to give more at life's
end. I believe when I give to the Lord, He can multiply it better than
I could if I were to keep it. So my thought has been, for many years,
to give — and *not* to build an estate. Our kids know there will be very
little left of our estate for them. They're OK. They have their own
estates." (They're co-owners with Paul and Ruth in the bank.)

Paul and Ruth do have an estate plan: part of it will continue to
provide for the 80 staff they support regularly, for five years after
their death. But other savings are not too tightly held. After Hurricane
Katrina, for instance, the Katrina Emergency Tax Act provided that

IRA funds could be donated completely tax-free to qualified charities. The Lindholms saw this as a great opportunity to transfer their 401K to an IRA and make a tax-free charitable deduction of the entire amount they'd saved over 50 years. It went primarily to Campus Crusade ministries.

Of course, they still pay substantial income tax at the state and federal levels, but they consider it good stewardship to make use of all deductions allowed by law to help those in need. Missions organizations are included as beneficiaries of all their retirement plans, and they've been tax-savvy in planning this, too. For instance, their U.S. savings bonds are specified in their will to go directly to missions, avoiding tax on the accrued interest. Two different accounting firms help them ensure they pay their appropriate taxes yet do the maximum possible in giving to ministries. That's exactly what we at The Great Commission Foundation help people do, so this was music to my ears ... as was Paul's positive attitude about it.

"I find such joy in giving, and find such joy in helping people come to know Jesus," Paul says. "I think the word *surrender* is a good word to use: to not live the 'self life,' but live the 'surrendered life' — because there is so much joy. Why would anyone want to focus on oneself and not the Lord?"

Chapter 9

— Randy and Sharon Conrads —

Big Hearts, Deep Pockets

I met Randy and Sharon Conrads because of their big hearts. They loved the Lord, and they wanted to make sure they were giving the most they could to His work. They didn't want any resources going to taxes that might instead be preserved for ministry. This kind of planning is what we do at The Great Commission Foundation, so I was happy to help them.

The Conradses seemed to be doing very well for themselves, but I could tell right away that this wasn't their focus. Whatever they did, they wanted to do it for the sake of the Kingdom of God.

Their main income was generated by the website Randy had founded, Classmates.com. It helps people connect with old school chums they may have lost track of, and it is quite popular. After helping Randy and Sharon make an estate plan that maximized charitable giving and minimized taxes, I added one word of advice: "Talk to me if you ever decide to sell your company. Capital gains tax is *optional* if we structure things correctly, and you could give major gifts to ministry, rather than paying taxes."

It's something I tell all the business owners I help through The Great Commission Foundation. Sometimes they do call me again — and Randy did. A corporation had made him a wonderful offer for Classmates.com, and he was considering selling. We worked together to help the Conradses make a charitable donation of their company's stock to a new Donor Advised Fund administered by The Great

Commission Foundation. The result was a substantial current-year charitable tax deduction, and when the company did sell, they avoided considerable capital gains taxes. This was an amazing moment for them, and for me. But it was really just the beginning of how Randy and Sharon would bless many ministries and missions with their generosity.

The sale of Classmates.com propelled Randy and Sharon from being people of some means to being truly wealthy. For many people who find themselves in such dramatically different circumstances — practically overnight — the change is too big, and it happens too fast. It leaves them completely unprepared for managing such wealth. Sadly, many rapidly lose their resources through over-spending. Some succumb to drug or alcohol abuse, or destroy their marriages and relationships. But the Conradses were already mature Christians. Their lives were focused on Jesus Christ. Their new financial status merely opened doors for them to do even more of His work.

"We realized we didn't need a lot of *things*," Randy says. "We were able to maintain a balanced lifestyle. And to give awesome amounts to Kingdom efforts like the Campus Ministry, EveryStudent.com, and our church."

High ROI is what the Conradses look for when they're considering their charitable giving.

"Evangelism and the resulting changed lives resonate with us,"

Randy says. "It's important to see results, so to me the reporting process is critical. I want personal interaction with the missionaries, evangelists, or project managers, to know what's in their hearts. And don't just tell me what you think I want to hear."

Because of his Internet expertise, many ministries ask Randy for advice about their own Web presence. If he's familiar with the outreach and the leadership, and he sees the potential for a good return, he's happy to help with advice ... but he'd prefer to be told upfront if his advice isn't going to be taken.

"One organization asked for my ideas on Web-based evangelism and growing their market. They were very complimentary and told me how great my ideas were, saying their team would be implementing them right away," Randy remembers. He was happy to help, and had even reserved a $1 million gift to help with the changes and development of the Internet outreach ... until he realized that, in fact, *none* of the ideas he'd offered were being used. All of his advice had been totally ignored, without explanation.

"They could have called and told me why they couldn't do what they'd said they would do," Randy says. "I might not have bought their reasoning, but at least they would have kept me informed, and kept the relationship alive, maybe kept the door open for future ministry projects together. The million dollars went instead to different ministries where I knew it would make an impact."

The Conradses feel the very ability to make charitable donations of such amounts is a gift from God, and they feel an obligation to invest wisely. One of Randy's favorite ways to give is through providing a lead gift for a matching challenge: for instance, donating $50,000 where there's a $100,000 need, and challenging other ministry supporters to provide the rest, so in effect their gifts will be doubled.

"It's even better to set the terms of the challenge so that the matching funds have to come in through 'new money,'" Randy adds. "Then the ministry team will get out and tell their story to new people who have never given before, rather than their regular supporters. That way, they not only reach the financial goal, but they get new supporters on board. It's a perfect way to leverage the original gift and multiply it."

This kind of partnership highlights for Randy and Sharon how they can make a difference in the world, working together with worthy ministries.

"They do their part in the field, and we do our part by investing our time and finances," Randy says. "We love to see people and projects become self-sustaining."

"We believe in the principle of laying up treasure in heaven," Sharon adds. "Eternity is a long time, so people should want to have more invested there than here. We're just trading earthly currency for heavenly currency — which are the souls of those who come to Christ because of our investment in ministry."

The couple's advice for anyone who has been blessed financially? "Malachi 3:10!" Randy says. "It's the only place in the Bible where we're actually told to test God! And what is the test? To bring your tithes and offerings, and trust Him to fulfill His promises, to open the windows of heaven and pour out a blessing. I don't know that God wants us to give with an expectation of receiving more in this life, but I've found it easy to take Him at His Word."

Chapter 10

John and Sue Roise

Dead Men
Don't Write Checks

"It doesn't take any faith for a dead man to give money away! Give it away now — that's how you exercise your faith."

John Roise's unorthodox truism might make some people a little uncomfortable — like me. After all, my work involves helping people discover how they can give their greatest gift to God's Kingdom; very often this is something that can only happen after they die: a life insurance policy, or an estate plan, may represent the only way. These vehicles for giving are very important, and they provide a lot of much-needed funding for ministries that are impacting the whole world. But is there something to what John Roise says? Is there a reason to give now, while you're living, rather than storing it up to give after you die?

Yes! For one thing, there's the joy you receive in your own life from the generosity you show. Why cheat yourself out of that excitement by waiting to give your best gifts until after you're gone? And then, as John's own story will show, there's the constant excitement of seeing where God will guide you next in your adventure of giving.

John had a secure career in the banking industry. Maybe it wouldn't sound too exciting to some people, but it was very good to John Roise. Sure, it could have seemed a little crazy for him to quit and launch his own business — but here's what you need to know about John: he has vision beyond banking. He wanted to devote his life to some important goals, including:

- Sharing his faith wherever he went. This was his passion — but as an employee of the bank, it did not seem right to use "bank time" for ministry purposes.

- Hiring people who needed a second chance: former drug addicts and felons, people who had made poor choices ... again, a bank is one of the last places these people would be welcomed as employees.

- Taking mission trips. John needed flexible scheduling to travel the world and share the love of God ... but a banker's schedule is less flexible.

- Speaking out on important issues of the day, such as abortion and pornography. A banker can't typically express opinions on such controversial topics.

It took faith to leave his job as a banker and transition to business owner ... because of the money. As a banker, he'd carried no personal debt and could count on a steady paycheck. As a business owner, he would be millions of dollars in debt, and he knew that steady income would only be possible when the business began to thrive.

"It was a step of faith," John says. "My wife Sue and I were completely trusting God."

Then just two years after making the transition they were introduced to the late Dr. Bill Bright, founder of Campus Crusade for Christ, and to the people of "History's Handful." These are men and women who have pledged to give $1 million to reach a million people with the good news of Jesus Christ. The Campus Crusade team had divided the world into Million People Target Areas (MPTAs) for the fulfillment of the Great Commission, and each $1 million pledged would provide strategic ministry to present the message of salvation to several MPTA groups.

"This was really more than I thought I could handle, especially since I was way in debt," John recalls. "We had a window company. How would God allow us to have the resources in this little window company so we could be involved in reaching all these people for Christ? It really put a new focus for us on our business."

John and Sue had never considered their business to be about making money for themselves. From the beginning, they had planned for the company to generate funds to advance God's Kingdom. The History's Handful challenge certainly seemed like a huge opportunity to do so — but they would have to trust God to provide.

"This was so exciting for us; it put a bounce in our step," John says. "No longer did the millions that we owed seem like a big thing. That was the beginning of how we committed to that first million dollars. And everything from then on was strategically directed toward how we could fund these Million People Target Areas."

The business philosophy was to hold profits loosely and invest them in ministry. John had seen in the banking industry that those who accumulated the most money and worldly possessions often seemed to be the least happy. He wasn't going to let that happen to him and Sue. As quickly as they generated profits, they donated them back into Kingdom work. Their commitment to a Christian project came before they had the money to fund the project. Through prayer, hard work and God's blessings they understood God would provide the funds that were needed. Their commitment came before they had the funds to fulfill their pledge.

"With that commitment," John says, "it was always hard when I made a business mistake, and I made several. It hurt, because with losses came the realization that we could not fund a new MPTA. Out of these mistakes — that should have been good deals but failed — came our strategy: *If something is not good, let it fail quick, let it fail cheap, get out, and shut it down!* A practice that we still abide by."

Giving generously was never a problem for the Roises, because they'd always been conscientious about tithing, and giving more than 10% whenever possible. Even back when they were first married and John was in the Army — making just $100 a month — they were givers. "I'd send all but $5 home to Sue each month," he recalls, "and she watched every penny. But the tithe always came out first. We gave it out of gratitude for how good God is, and the knowledge that everything comes from Him. It was just recognition of all that God had given us, and the knowledge that every opportunity is from Him."

The opportunity to leave the banking industry and go into the window business turned out to be a tremendously wise move for John. It helped him fulfill the goals he had set for himself, and gave him and Sue the ability to bless many Kingdom ministries with their generous investments. But their constant giving has left very little in their own bank account. And on their company's balance sheet, they show few liquid assets. They don't have complex financial statements because they own the company — and they found out recently that the company has limited bonding because it appears on paper to have so few liquid assets.

"This brings up a temptation for me to put some money away, just in case we have to apply for a bond," John says. "I argue with myself, that I do not want to bank a pile of money, because — what if God calls me home tomorrow and I'm sitting there with a bank account full of money? That is not being very faithful!"

Faithfulness is the key for John and Sue, and for their son Geoff as well.

"If you have a big balance sheet, what's it for?" John asks. "Modestly take care of yourself and your immediate family, but after that give it away, liquidate. As long as I have the ability to give (working or retired), this is what I will do. And our son Geoff's heart is the same as ours. Let's get this thing moving, earn some resources, and see how quickly we can give it away!"

Their motto: "Just because we *can* doesn't mean we *should*."

Just because they could afford something nicer, something better, something newer for themselves doesn't mean they ought to go out and buy it. "I drive a PT Cruiser which I bought in 2000; it's 10 years old. But you know, it gets me around just fine," John says. "Someday I will get a different car, but for now it works for me. New cars, a bigger house, those things are not important. We live comfortably. Can we afford to live somewhere else? Yes, but we are very happy with what we have. God has been good to us — and the less we spend on ourselves, the more we can give away. When God provides more, we don't want to improve our 'standard of living,' but we want to increase our 'standard of giving.' We know contentment is not dependent on money — 1 Tim 6:6-10, 17-19.

A lifestyle of sacrifice and generosity brings the Roise family great joy — and they're always careful to watch for the ROI, too. Global Media Outreach is a ministry they support because the statistics show that for every $2, 3 people indicate decisions for Christ. "Where can you find a better return on investment than that?!" John asks with delight.

This kind of return is the "real story" of John and Sue's balance sheet. When their banker told them the constant giving made their books look thin — and he suggested they invest in stocks, bonds, and other liquid assets to bulk them up — John replied that he wished his banker could see the "other set of books." The banker was shocked. A separate set of books?

"My real balance sheet is showing in heaven," John told him, "where the investments are for eternity; and I am going to see those. These are all gifts from the Maker who gave me these resources. I'm going to see Him; so my rewards are there in heaven."

John's goal is to send on ahead of him, into eternity, all the resources he can. His advice to all believers is this: "Give it away while you are living, because that takes faith. Those who can write that big check should do it. And then see the exciting journey that God takes you on, to give more, and overcome the fear. It takes no faith to give something away when you are dead. Give it away while you are living, because that takes faith." It also takes faith to make a commitment before you have the money and then pray, plan, work hard and watch God provide.

I'm still excited about helping people to arrange their estate planning advantageously from a tax standpoint, or to direct their life insurance policy into ministry ... but I think John has a point here. There's no reason to die with your bank account bloated, when you could joyfully give it all away — and die broke ... knowing you invested it all in God's Kingdom!

Mathew 25:21

Chapter 11

Ron and Cristy Varela

Making Lemonade

Crash!

It was the sound of the global economy collapsing on everyone. Particularly in the USA, on anyone involved in the real estate or development business.

Ron and Cristy Varela were hit hard.

In years past, they'd joyfully given charitable contributions which many of us might consider immense — God had blessed their business, and they wanted to be a blessing to others in return. Their great hearts for ministry led them to help Campus Crusade for Christ, Pinnacle Forum, Latin American Council, Advocates for Faith and Freedom, and missions in Ecuador, Guatemala, Bolivia, and Brazil.

Their support for these outreaches wasn't all monetary, either. They loved to go and pour themselves into ministry. Their first mission trip with Campus Crusade was as part of "Maximizers" in Ecuador; this group targets businesspeople and industry leaders for evangelism by connecting them with successful Christian businesspeople in the USA for conferences, seminars, and valuable personal interactions. Ron and Cristy, with their group, knew they would be part of these conferences, but had no idea how important their presence would become. They met with leaders in industry and banking and with construction company owners and managers. They took part in seminars with 800 business leaders over the course of just a few days. And they were exhilarated to see how the Gospel message was woven into lessons about business ethics and productivity.

"We were going 100 miles an hour the whole time," Cristy recalls. "It was wonderful. It was exciting."

"There is a lot of corruption in many Latin countries; it's just accepted," Ron says. "I think those businesspeople and leaders were tired of this way of business and banking. They just wanted to make a difference, and they were surprised to learn that the principles Maximizers taught were from the Bible."

Maximizer staff follow up on each of the conference and seminar attendees, so those who want to know more about Jesus, or who came to Christ during the outreach, can continue growing in the faith — and continue maximizing their business, too.

Before the Varelas' interaction with Campus Crusade, they had never thought about stewardship and what it could really mean: that all they had came from God, and there was a joy to be found in giving it back to Him. Then they began to partner with Campus Crusade in Military Ministry and found themselves meeting with high-ranking military leaders and police officials in Latin America to share the love of Jesus Christ.

Giving their money and their time to these ministries was a great blessing for the Varelas, whose land development business had been hugely successful; it even allowed them to purchase a 3,000-acre ranch in Arizona where Cristy could daily ride her beloved horses. But then the economy crashed, and their business became much less lucrative in a very short time. No longer could they afford mission trips to Latin America or large gifts to the ministries they loved. They're still quite active in giving and ministry; people like the Varelas don't just *stop giving*, no matter what their circumstances. But they felt their reduced giving wasn't accurately portraying the generosity of their souls, or their deep gratitude to God.

To some, losing such great amounts of income might have seemed a bitter disappointment. Others may have questioned: *God, we were giving so much to Your work; why are we now caught in this financial crisis?*

But the Varelas responded differently.

They continued to give faithfully from whatever God placed in their hands (which is still no small amount), and then they decided to do even more, with the home and property God had given them. They had witnessed firsthand how hard Campus Crusade staff and other ministry leaders and missionaries work when they're on the field — and they knew these people would benefit tremendously by coming to a place where they could relax and recharge, maybe ride horses or go hiking.

They opened their ranch home as a retreat for Christian ministries and groups. This tranquil oasis in the desert is worth just as much — to missionaries, ministers, and other believers — as any monetary gift they have given. It provides a beautiful place for relaxation and renewal, for prayer and meditation, and for weary souls to become revitalized and recharged for more effective ministry.

"This gave us a different view of our property," Ron says. "What would God want us to do for His glory? What is the next step? How do we do this? Who do we invite to retreats? We began to pray about these questions."

"It's something we can do for the Lord, and it does not take a lot of cash," Cristy says. "We appreciate so much what missionaries and other Christian workers do, and we know that balance is hard to achieve when you're passionate in that role.... It can be hard to find rest."

Their ranch retreat is the perfect setting for passionate Christian leaders and missionaries to go "off the grid" for a while and find that peace and rest. Recently missionary Armando Tomayo stayed for a few days — and he says it was one of his most memorable trips ever.

Ron and Cristy thank God for what He's doing through them. Yes, life handed them lemons: an economic downturn that, for the moment, prevents them from giving as much money and time on the mission field as they would really like to give. But the Varelas have gone far beyond the proverbial step of making lemonade.

"To use what God has already given us is wonderful," Ron says. "We are so glad to give rest and refreshment to ministry people so that they can go back into the world to do what needs to be done for Christ."

It doesn't take a million dollars to make a difference.

Sometimes it just takes a gift of hospitality, given with grace and love.

Chapter 12

—— *Skip & Sharon Ast* ——

A Life-Giving Legacy

She was leaving him!

Skip Ast's high school sweetheart, Sharon, had joined the Marines. He understood. Her childhood hadn't been happy, and she wanted out of this town. He would wait for her, at least until her tour of duty ended. But then, a shock: she had been accepted for Officers Candidate School. She could become career military. Suddenly Skip knew — if he wanted to keep that girl, he had to marry her. He asked her to leave the military and become his wife.

Soon, the couple had children, but Skip saw no conflict between fatherhood and partying every night. He stayed out late, drank up paychecks, got into bar fights, and had horrific arguments with his wife at home, too.

Until she stopped arguing with him. When Sharon Ast chose to follow Christ as Savior, she was like a new woman, a new wife, a new mom. She wouldn't take the bait when Skip came home stumbling drunk. Instead, she would welcome him home and fix his dinner. She quietly and efficiently raised the children, kept the house, and spent most of her spare time in Bible study. If Skip had been scared she would leave him back when she was considering Officers Candidate School, he was terrified now. He was losing her to God.

His new plan? He would claim to be a Christian as well! He started going to church with the family. He even went through confirmation classes. But whatever transformation had seized Sharon had yet to seize Skip.

"During the week, I continued to feed my addictions," Skip says. "Then on Sunday I became a good, church-going family man. I had become something I always despised: a hypocrite."

He knew his dual life wasn't enough to save his marriage. Sharon was growing closer to God all the time, while Skip remained on the outside looking in.

"I prepared myself mentally and emotionally to lose my wife and family, whom I loved very much," Skip recalls.

But at this critical crossroads, Skip and Sharon were invited to a Lay Institute for Evangelism sponsored by Campus Crusade for Christ. That night, Founder Bill Bright was speaking.

"He said Jesus Christ died on the cross for everyone's sins," Skip remembers, "and unless you were washed in the blood of Christ, you couldn't have a personal relationship with Him. One part of my mind recoiled at the thought of being washed in anyone's blood. I knew what this meant. I arrived home many nights after a fight in a bar, covered in somebody else's blood, and it repulsed me. But another part of my mind said, *Skip, this is missing link in your life.*"

He had done all he could do to salvage his life and marriage, and it wasn't working. So despite the inner dialogue that told him he couldn't really believe in all this religious nonsense, Skip chose to pray the prayer with Dr. Bright — and truly give his life to Christ.

"I said those words, and I meant them," Skip says. "It was the greatest experience I ever had, receiving Christ in my heart."

A new value system was born inside Skip, and in his family. He compares it to the words of 2 Corinthians 5:17: "Therefore, if anyone *is* in Christ, *he is* a new creation; old things have passed away; behold, all things have become new." Everything became new for Skip and Sharon Ast: their spiritual lives, their family....

And their business, too.

Skip, his brother, and a local pool builder launched their own pool company in Phoenix. Within two years, Shasta Industries became the area's #1 pool builder. In 1967, their first year of business, they built 225 pools. Today Shasta has eight divisions, eight executives, 300 employees; and they've built thousands of pools and by God's grace, achieved the #1 position as an independent pool builder internationally.

"We want to astonish our customers and use the business as a way of influencing people every day to establish a personal relationship with Jesus Christ," Skip says. The funds and influence that come with such a successful business are also being used to share the Gospel message around the world, through Skip and Sharon's personal ministries, and through their significant investment in Campus Crusade for Christ and other outreaches.

"The most significant, pivotal point in my Christian adventure came in November of 1972," Skip says. "I was invited to a retreat sponsored by Campus Crusade for Christ. During this retreat, I was very touched to hear the then-Chairman of Holiday Inn speak about how God had enabled him to give a large sum to Campus Crusade in order to help change the world, through supernaturally changed lives. I knew in that moment I had discovered God's purpose for calling me into the business world!"

Dr. Bright had challenged everyone at the retreat: "Do something significant with your life." There was a form to fill out and a check-box to mark for more information about an adventure in giving. Skip checked the box, and Dr. Bright's office called to set an appointment ... Skip was sure he would be asked for a major contribution — what would it be, $10,000... or even $25,000? He was astounded when he was again challenged to do something significant with his life — and give a quarter-million dollars to reach and disciple lost souls with the person, Jesus Christ. Skip immediately felt he wanted to do it, to live a life of significance. And although he didn't have the $250,000 available, he stepped forward in faith and gave $50,000 to start. When he and Sharon fulfilled the pledge months later, they were so excited. Skip called Dr. Bright and asked, "What else is there for us to do?"

Today, Skip says, "Dr. Bright made that seemingly impossible challenge, but it pulled me out of my self-contained world and got me to stretch out and believe I could do something significant with my life that would honor God and glorify Jesus Christ. I realized I was now driven to reach and disciple the lost. That excitement is a huge part of our lives today."

Skip and Sharon — and their company, Shasta Pools — have given significantly to sponsor 17 MPTAs (Million People Target Areas) reaching more than 17 million people worldwide with the Gospel. In fact, every employee of the company knows that sharing the story of Jesus is why the company exists. They share in the fruit of this great evangelistic effort.

Skip and Sharon Ast feel privileged to be stewards of their time and resources. "We want to be 'owners of nothing and stewards of everything,'" Skip says. "These days I am not as concerned about my legacy as I am that everyone has the opportunity to come to know Christ in a personal way."

Lately, business has slowed down because of the general economic conditions across the country, and the Asts find themselves unable to give at the same level as before. Although Skip finds this disheartening, he was encouraged when his friend Dave Hannah recently reminded him of all the people they had reached for Christ and the work that continues to multiply and grow today: "God understands that — you need to remember there are thousands and thousands of people who have come to Christ out there because of your giving, who are sharing the Gospel and discipling others right now. Your giving has an ongoing legacy and multiplies even in those times when you are not able to give." His heart was lifted to see the synergy of seeds sown over 38 years and a harvest that continues until Jesus returns.

The couple's business success, success as a family, and success in presenting the Gospel to millions all over the world are all credited to Jesus Christ and the transforming work He has done in their lives, and Skip adds these important ideas for anyone who wants to make an impact on their family and their world through their business:

- Trust God with everything you do, and put Him first in your life. It's impossible to be a failure (no matter the appearances) if you have truly put Christ in first place in your life.
- Live by a set of Scriptual values and God's plan for your life will lead you. Skip has seen his family business grow and thrive because of the godly values enforced in the workplace, and in his life.
- In business, implement a company mission that employees can whole-heartedly embrace. For instance, Shasta Industries' mission statement is: "We are dedicated to creating distinctive pools, innovative products, and astonishing services through effective process improvement and aggressive execution.
- Work like it all depends on you, *pray* like it all depends on God (James 2:17) — and do unto others as you would have them do unto you (Matthew 7:12).
- Give to charitable organizations, and build a business that's a part

of the community.

God has blessed Skip and Sharon's marriage, family, and business as they've learned to live by these guidelines, and in turn, they've blessed many ministries, missions organizations, and people in need. What a wonderful legacy!

2 Corinthians 5:17

Chapter 13

——— Ted and Geneva Servais ———

What Would Jesus Do?

KINGDOM GIVING, A NEW PERSPECTIVE ON WEALTH

What would Jesus do? This is a question that Ted and Geneva ask regularly as they look for worthy ministry opportunities to invest in. In fact, my first conversation with Geneva was in response to her research on projects she had discovered that she felt God was using — and which she believed might benefit by some funding she felt led to give.

Over the years, I have talked with Geneva and Ted as they shared their desire to reach people for Christ. They are patient and focused and very purposeful in their giving. This must come from years of hard work with their eyes on the goal.

Ted Servais was a young entrepreneur when he met Geneva. He had a successful rug cleaning business in Los Angeles; but as he confides in me, it was after Geneva joined him as wife (and business manager) that the business really took off. Ted's real dream was to retire by age 40, through wise real estate investing. He actually did it ahead of schedule, Geneva informed me (and there was no mistaking the pride and love in her eyes).

But how could a man with so much energy just retire? He couldn't — instead he dabbled in other businesses, and then in his spare time started taking in a few rugs to clean in the garage. This "retirement" business grew so rapidly, Geneva lobbied for Ted to move it out of the garage and into its own premises. He bought another building on the main street in Newport Beach, California, and quickly built a second thriving carpet cleaning business with 11 trucks, 20 employees, and all the things that he had retired from!

Of course, Ted and Geneva do more than work hard. They also play hard. Even the way they first met was fun — Ted was buying a boat, and the way it turned out, he ended up with Geneva's boat — *and* Geneva. They both love the water. Geneva once took the challenge to race on water skis, from L.A. to Catalina Island, and back. She did it in 2½ hours. Other recreation activities they've enjoyed? Flying their own plane up the coast — or down to Mexico to play tennis — spending weekends on the beach or in the mountains. They've made the most of every leisure moment they've had.

But this life was, truth be told, a little shallow for them — until a friend invited them to church, and they discovered the love and grace of Jesus Christ. Prior to that, Ted says, they used to drive by the church and wave, but they had "Sunday things" to do. In time they started attending church and felt they had all their bases covered, though no dramatic change in their lives occurred. But then by "random chance," as they put it, they met David Wilkerson, the founder of Teen Challenge, now World Challenge. He was attending an RV show in Phoenix, Arizona, where they were exhibiting their new motor coach. He invited them to a meeting where he would be speaking, in Palm Springs, California.

"We realized after the meeting started that it was for pastors and their wives," Geneva recalls, "but we were in the front row. We couldn't just get up and walk out."

At the first break, Brother Dave, as he is known, came straight from the podium to greet them and welcome them to stay. In fact, he said to them, "You don't know it yet, but God has anointed you for His service." This meeting, this prophecy, caused them to realize that following Jesus was more than just attending church. It was a turning point for them — and they got serious with God. They began to look for ways to be involved in God's work. It was the beginning of their "journey into giving."

At first, the Servais simply began by sharing the Gospel with Bibles and books. They gave them away wherever they went. Later, they began investing in worthy ministries. Geneva remembers she felt she was working all the time, and yet they had enough money to live well. She decided if she were going to work, it would be for Jesus.

They heard about tithing but never felt limited to giving one-tenth of their income. "Whatever we have, over what we need to live on," Ted says, "is available for God to direct." Today they routinely give away about half of their income.

The Servais take great joy in giving, but they like to give responsibly. They want to know that the money is used well, reaching the most people possible. They watch personal spending and expect ministries and missionaries to do the same.

They heard about the JESUS Film Project years ago and stopped in

WHAT WOULD JESUS DO?

at the Campus Crusade offices in San Bernardino to check it out. Paul Eshleman, the man God used in the amazing growth and outreach of the JESUS Film, gave them a tour and explained the exciting success of the film in introducing people to Jesus and launching new churches. Ted and Geneva were hooked. They immediately purchased some projectors for missionaries to take the Gospel to unreached people. But this was just the beginning. They have since provided translations, supported missionaries, and published a number of books for Dr. Bright.

Ted and Geneva have invested through the years in many ministries, including Joni and Friends, Turning Point with Dr. David Jeremiah, Open Doors (getting Bibles behind the Iron Curtain), and church-planting in Romania, Uganda, and elsewhere. Of course, they're actively involved in their church, Calvary Chapel, with Pastor Chuck Smith.

With all the various projects and ministries they've supported, some have not turned out as planned. "A couple of situations turned out to be more of a learning experience than anything else," Ted admits. But the couple has faithfully sown the Gospel through responsible ministries that help them fulfill God's call on their lives. Ted states emphatically that he and Geneva have a specific ministry: "to bring as many people to the Lord as possible" (Mark 16:15).

The Servais have worked and played hard all their lives, and they give with the same passion, intensity, and joy. It's a delight to see the twinkle in Geneva's eyes when she feels the Lord directing her to be involved in a new project for Him. She and Ted enjoy the adventure of doing what Jesus would do!

Chapter 14

— Frank and Charri Sutherlin —

You Guessed It...

"Ideally, if I really knew the future, I would like to die broke."

By now, you're probably not surprised to read these words. Quite a number of people have expressed the same sentiment. Frank and Charri Sutherlin, too. They've made a habit of generous giving, and Frank is among those who just can't wait to die completely penniless.

"I would like to have invested everything in the Kingdom."

He didn't always feel that way. He always went to church, of course, but it wasn't until he lost his first wife to cancer that he began to be convicted about his love of money. A widower with two children in high school and two children in pre-school, he began seeing life through God's eyes, praying earnestly every day for His guidance and help. The Lord brought Charri into his life, and a year later they were married.

But then — Frank again looked death in the face.

He was diagnosed with cancer.

"I thought I was going to die. I had seen my wife die," Frank says. "All posturing and pretense evaporated. At this point, you have to get real honest with yourself. *How have I used my life?* You think about the end of your life, and the end of opportunities to do anything for God and eternity. You look back and say, *what a waste. So I earned a lot of money? Now I'm going to die, and what did I do with that money?*"

Frank determined that he would not look back from the end of his life at a mountain of money with no meaning.

The diagnosis of non-Hodgkin's lymphoma was good news and bad news, according to his doctor: it was generally treatable with radiation, but it might also come back. When Frank had undergone the treatment and was pronounced cancer-free, he knew that it wasn't a *cure*; and that knowledge, he says, has kept him on his knees. He is a man of prayer who is serious about making his life count; and his second wife, Charri, is in complete agreement.

Frank's business is real estate, and God has blessed his investments in many ways. He had four children with his first wife, three more with Charri, and they're in the process of adopting three orphaned sisters from China. The couple has been generous with their children, but Frank qualifies that assessment: "We gave them the opportunity to go to college and a good basis to make their own living, but I don't want to make them derelicts; I don't want to destroy their incentive." The children have invested their own money in various projects with their dad, and he's happy to help them that way ... but these days he and Charri are looking for an eternal return on their biggest investments.

"I look at the JESUS Film Project, and you get a lot of bang for your buck!" Frank exclaims. "I look at the return on the dollar — my investment mentality — and I look at what it costs to bring people to the Lord. I think that is the most fruitful investment out there, considering the number of people reached per dollar."

His enthusiasm for the JESUS Film is boundless, but he invests in other ministries, too — particularly focusing on East Asia — with great joy.

"What piqued our interest in East Asia was this idea that you could build a church for $6,000 or $10,000," Frank says. "There's an explosion of new Christians and no facilities — and you can build a church for 600 people, including the land and even the parsonage. That was a great return on investment from a real estate standpoint."

Recently, the Sutherlins have visited East Asia to see three churches built through their generosity (they have funded more than two dozen church projects). They've also been to China (to see two of the children they're adopting), and to India to visit a missionary they support in a leper colony. On the same trip, they visited Cambodia, where they are funding a radio tower and transmitter to reach the entire country.

"The lepers have been praying for us for years, because they know we help provide for them," Frank says. "And although 'leper colonies' was not high on our list of places to visit, what a privilege to see the work this missionary is doing, and meet these Christians who have been praying for us."

For Frank, however, such experiences are just icing on the cake. What really gets him going is seeing how far a dollar invested in ministry will go — and thinking about the eternal impact he's making.

"Most of my life has been all about *getting*; if other people are like me, they want to get a home, a car, an education, good investments, a retirement plan; these are all part of the American Dream," Frank says.

"But there is a point at which you have to realize that these are all *short-term* investments, and you really want a *long-term* investment. Let me define what I think of short-term: it is what you invest in this lifetime, usually 100 years or less. Long-term investments are for eternity, and that's one life on top of another, 100 years on top of another 100 years on top of another 100 years. When you really get the perspective of eternity, then you will be more motivated to plan for eternity, and invest in eternity."

Frank and Charri have obviously grasped the idea of investing in eternity. They donate about 60% of their income to charitable organizations. While they live well, they don't spend extravagantly. They live in a tract home rather than a gated community. Frank drives a 1996 Suburban. Although they could afford a newer car, he figures this one is still getting him where he needs to go.

"Giving away and getting rid of assets is almost un-American — it's the unwritten rule that nobody talks about," Frank says.

"We are all mortal, we will all die — which was driven home when my first wife of 19 years died at the age of 41, and then when I got cancer. The question, as stated by Randy Alcorn, is: 'As I move toward eternity, am I moving closer to my treasures or further away from my treasures?' If we have invested in God's Kingdom as we move closer to the end, we are moving closer to our treasures — because they have been sent on ahead."

So in a way, Frank and Charri won't really be dying broke.

They'll be awakening to more treasure than they could ever have imagined.

Afterword

By Jerry Wear

The people you have heard from in this book have discovered something marvelous — something very few people can lay claim to:

They've discovered the joy, the excitement, of giving — the adventure of living with purpose!

They are outside the box in terms of their passion and philosophy of work, ministry, and giving. Many give over 50% of their income to ministry. You've read of several who have a plan to decrease their net worth systematically as they give, not just from their income, but from their capital, too.

Each of these entrepreneurs made an important discovery that changed their lives. They came to understand that God has gifted them in business and finance. One day, each realized there was a higher purpose for their talent than competing in the marketplace, keeping score with income and net worth.

Each realized their work is where their ministry *starts*. They are using their God-given ability to manage God-given income, assets, and opportunities to accomplish God-directed results. This is true stewardship.

Every day, these energetic entrepreneurs go to work to do the best with their abilities, not to grow the bank account or net worth statement

... they would consider that to be trivial when they have Kingdom work to do. Kingdom work is the passion that motivates them.

But here's a secret: Even if they're successful in giving it *all* away, they can never really die broke. Their heavenly balance sheet, reflecting the millions of souls won to Christ because of the ministries they supported, make them more rich than Solomon ever dreamed. It's a legacy they can never lose. It has already preceded them to heaven!

I pray that their stories have inspired you to do what they have done, to discover the joy of giving, the excitement of living with purpose — to step out in faith and enjoy the adventure God has for you.

There's a gripping scene in the Zeffirelli film *Brother Sun, Sister Moon*. St. Francis is being dragged to the judge by his father. His father wants him declared insane because he's giving away all his possessions — Dad wants to protect Francis' fortune from his own charitable tendencies. But young Francis declares:

Father! I want to share the joy with you. Our treasures are in heaven, not here on earth! Don't be a slave of these! Throw it all away! Do as I do, it's so simple, be free!

To Francis, the madness is *not* giving everything away, but clinging *to* things. In giving it all away, he finds freedom ... and amazingly, he finds it *easy* to let go.

Do you hear his cry? Do you see how, in the wonderful paradox of the Kingdom, giving away your earthly treasure buys for you an eternal treasure in heaven?

If you've caught this vision, then it's time to do as St. Francis did, as all the people in these pages are doing, and begin giving it away. Break the bonds of material things and discover the freedom of living by Kingdom rules.

"It's so simple, *be free!*"

If we at The Great Commission Foundation can help you do it, remember we're here for you.

The Great Commission Foundation of
Campus Crusade for Christ
100 Lake Hart Dr, #3600
Orlando, FL 32832
p: 800.449.5454
e: info@gcfccc.org
www.gcfccc.org